AUTHENTIC CHORDS
ORIGINAL KEYS
COMPLETE SONGS

Elvis!

GREATEST HITS

Cover photo © ELVIS PRESLEY ENTERPRISES, INC.
Arranged by Steven Smith and Michael Walsh

ISBN 0-634-02824-3

HAL•LEONARD®
CORPORATION

7777 W. BLUEMOUND RD. P.O. BOX 13819 MILWAUKEE, WI 53213

www.elvis-presley.com

Visit Hal Leonard Online at
www.halleonard.com

CONTENTS

All Shook Up

Words and Music by Otis Blackwell and Elvis Presley

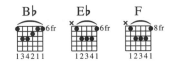

Intro

Moderate Shuffle

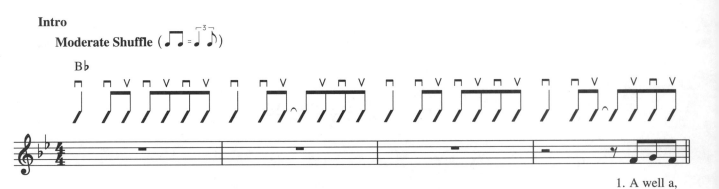

1. A well a,

Verse

bless my soul, __ what's wrong with me? __ I'm itch-ing like a man __ on a fuz-zy tree. __ My
2. *See Additional Lyrics*

friends say I'm act-in' wild as a bug. __ I'm in love. I'm all shook up! __ Mm, __

mm, ooh, ooh, yeah, __ yeah, __ yeah! __ 2. A-well my

Bridge

___ Well, please __ don't ask __ me what's a on my mind, __ I'm a
See Additional Lyrics

lit - tle mixed up but I feel fine. __ When I'm near that girl __ that I love best __ my heart beats so it scares me to death! When she touched __ my hand, what a chill I got. __ Her lips are like __ a vol - ca - no that's hot! I'm __ proud to say that she's my but - ter - cup. I'm in love! I'm all shook up. __ Mm, __ mm, ooh, ooh, yeah, __

Outro

1. __ yeah, __ yeah! __ My __ yeah, __ yeah! __ Mm, __
2. mm, ooh, ooh, yeah, __ yeah, __ I'm all shook up!

Additional Lyrics

2. A well, my hands are shaky and my knees are weak.
I can't seem to stand on my own two feet.
Who do you thank when you have such luck?
I'm in love. I'm all shook up! Mm, mm, ooh, ooh, yeah, yeah, yeah!

Bridge My tongue gets tied when I try to speak.
My insides shake like a leaf on a tree.
There's only one cure for this soul of mine.
That's to have the girl that I love so fine!

Always on My Mind

Words and Music by Wayne Thompson, Mark James and Johnny Christopher

Additional Lyrics

2. Maybe I didn't hold you
   All those lonely, lonely times,
   And I guess I never told you
   I'm so happy that you're mine.
   If I made you feel second best,
   Girl, I'm so sorry I was blind.

Are You Lonesome Tonight?

Words and Music by Roy Turk and Lou Handman

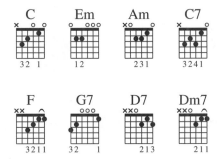

Do the chairs in your par- lor _____ seem emp - ty _____ and bare? Do you

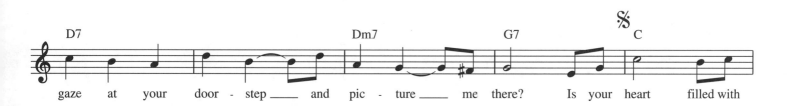

gaze at your door - step _____ and pic - ture _____ me there? Is your heart filled with

To Coda ⊕

pain, shall I come back _____ a - gain? Tell me, dear, are you lone - some _____ to -

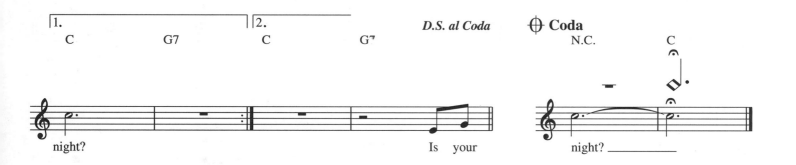

1. C   G7   **2.** C   G7   ***D.S. al Coda***   ⊕ **Coda**   N.C.   C

night?   Is your   night? _____

Additional Lyrics

Recitation: *I wonder if you're lonesome tonight.*
      You know, someone said that the world's a stage and each must play a part.
      Fate had me playing in love with you as my sweetheart.
      Act one was where we met; I loved you at first glance.
      You read your lines so cleverly and never missed a cue.
      Then came act two, you seemed to change; you acted strange and why I've never known.
      Honey, you lied when you said you loved me,
      And I had no cause to doubt you.
      But I'd rather go on hearing your lies,
      Than to go on living without you.
      Now the stage is bare and I'm standing there with emptiness all around.
      And if you won't come back to me, then they can bring the curtain down.

Blue Suede Shoes

Words and Music by Carl Lee Perkins

uh - uh, hon-ey, lay off ___ them shoes and don't ___ you step on my blue suede

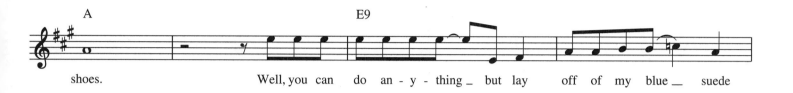

shoes. Well, you can do an-y-thing ___ but lay off of my blue ___ suede

Guitar Solo

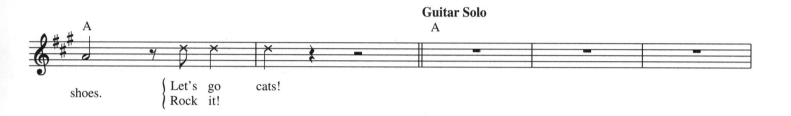

shoes. Let's go cats! / Rock it!

|1. |2. *D.S. al Coda*

3. Well, you can 4. Well, it's a -

✚ **Coda**

Outro

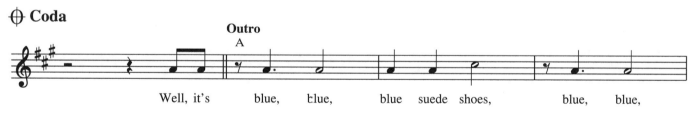

Well, it's blue, blue, blue suede shoes, blue, blue,

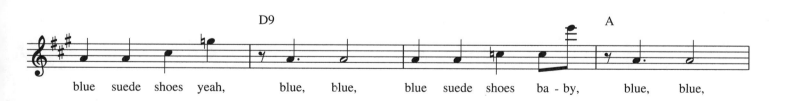

blue suede shoes yeah, blue, blue, blue suede shoes ba-by, blue, blue,

blue suede shoes. Well, you can do an-y-thing ___ but lay off ___ of my ___ blue suede shoes.

Burning Love

Words and Music by Dennis Linde

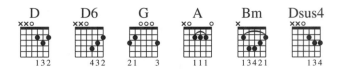

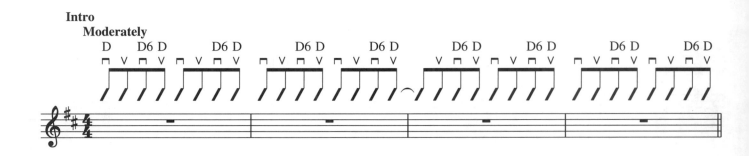

Intro
Moderately

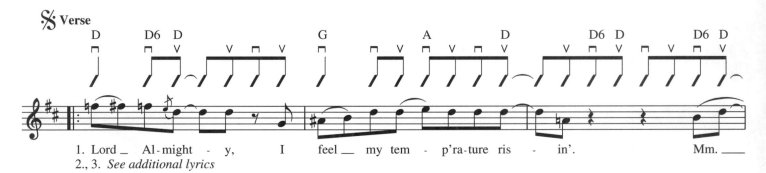

1. Lord __ Al-might-y, I feel __ my tem - p'ra-ture ris - in'. Mm. __
2., 3. *See additional lyrics*

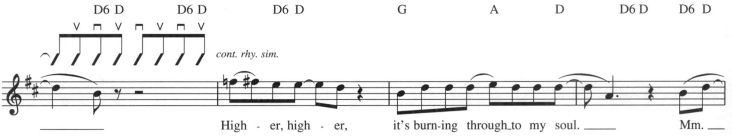

cont. rhy. sim.

High - er, high - er, it's burn-ing through to my soul. ____ Mm. __

Girl, __ girl, __ girl, girl, you gone and set __ me on fire. __ Mm.

My brain __ is flam - in', I don't know which __ way to go. ____ Yeah. __

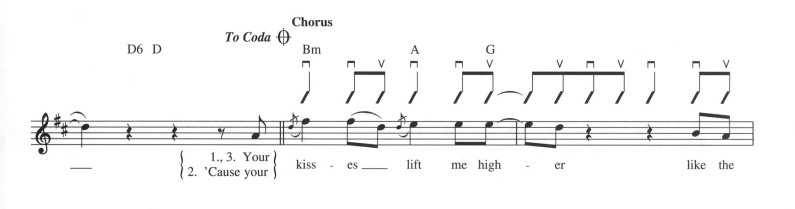

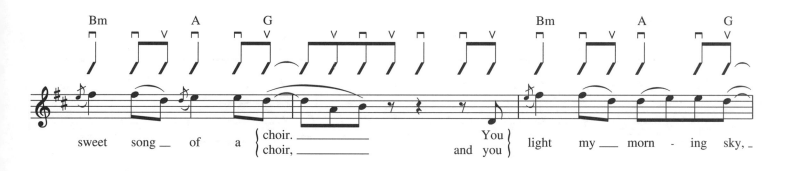

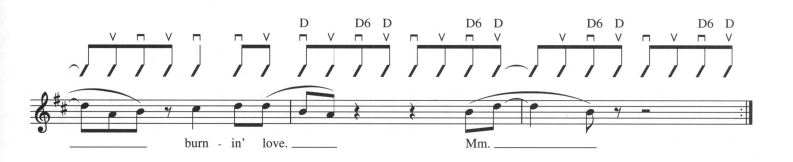

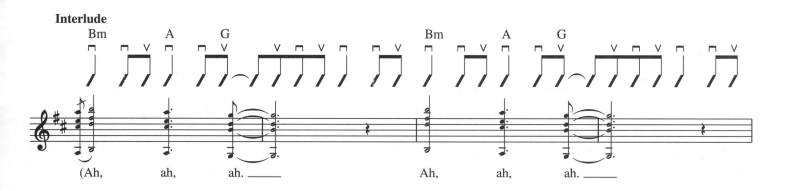

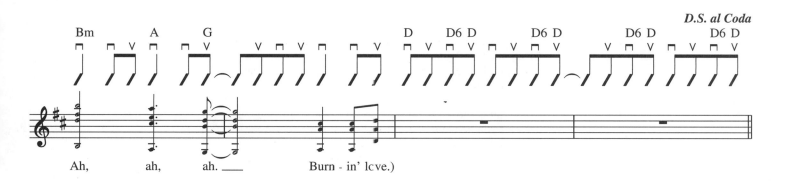

⊕ **Coda**
Chorus

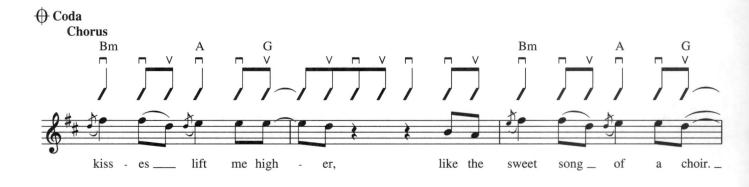

kiss - es ___ lift me high - er, like the sweet song ___ of a choir.

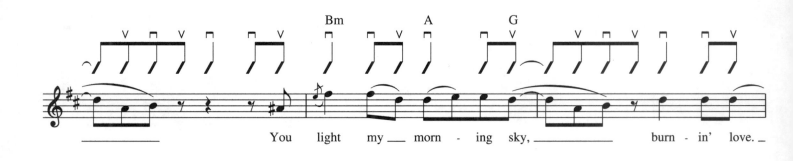

___ You light my ___ morn - ing sky, ___ burn - in' love. ___

___ Ah, burn - in' love. ___ I'm just a

Outro

Repeat and fade

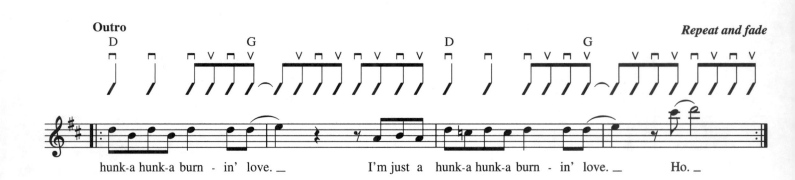

hunk-a hunk-a burn - in' love. _ I'm just a hunk-a hunk-a burn - in' love. _ Ho. _

Additional Lyrics

2. Hoo, hoo, hoo. I feel my temp'rature risin', mm.
   Help me I'm flamin', I must be a hundred and nine, mm.
   Burnin', burnin', burnin', and nothin' can cool me, yeah.
   I just might turn to smoke, but I feel fine.

3. It's comin' closer, the flames are now lickin' my body, mm.
   Won't you help me? I feel like I'm slippin' away, yeah.
   It's hard to breathe, my chest is heaving, mm, mm.
   Lord have mercy, I'm burnin' a hole where I lay, yeah.

Can't Help Falling in Love

Words and Music by George David Weiss, Hugo Peretti and Luigi Creatore

Additional Lyrics

2. Shall I stay?
   Would it be a sin
   If I can't help falling in love with you?

Don't

Words and Music by Jerry Leiber and Mike Stoller

Verse
Slowly

1. "Don't, don't," that's what you say ___ each
2., 3. *See additional lyrics*

time that I hold ___ you this ___ way. When I feel like

this and I want ___ to kiss you, ba - by, don't say, "don't." "don't."

Bridge

If you think that this is just a game I'm play - ing, ___

D.C. al Coda

if you think that I don't mean ___ ev - 'ry word I'm say - ing....

Coda

won't. Ba - by, don't say "don't."

Additional Lyrics

2. Don't, don't leave my embrace.
For here in my arms is your place.
When the night grows cold and I want to hold you,
Baby, don't say "don't."

3. Don't, don't, don't feel that way.
I'm your love and yours I will stay.
This you can believe, I will never leave you.
Heaven knows I won't.
Baby, don't say, "don't."

Heartbreak Hotel

Words and Music by Mae Boren Axton, Tommy Durden and Elvis Presley

Verse
Moderately slow

1. Well, since my __ ba - by left me well, I found a new place to dwell. Well, it's
though it's __ al - ways crowd - ed, you still can find some room for

down at the end __ of Lone - ly Street at Heart - break Ho - tel __ where I'll be,
brok - en heart - ed lov - ers to cry there in the gloom. __ We'll be so,

I'll be so lone - ly, ba - by, well, I'm so lone - ly,
we'll be so lone - ly, ba - by, well, we'll be so lone - ly,

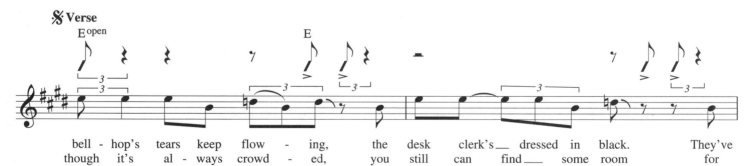

I'll be so lone - ly __ I could die. 2. Al -
well, they're so lone - ly __ they could die. 3. Now, the

Verse

bell - hop's tears keep flow - ing, the desk clerk's __ dressed in black. They've
though it's al - ways crowd - ed, you still can find __ some room for

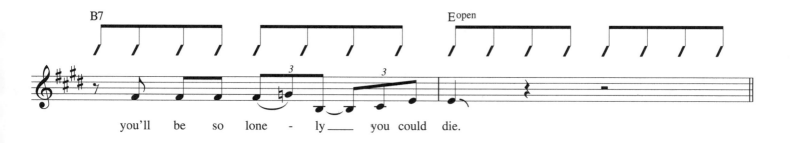

you'll be so lone - ly ____ you could die.

Guitar Solo

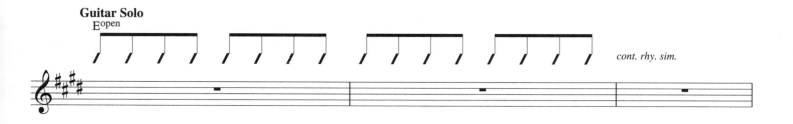

cont. rhy. sim.

Piano Solo

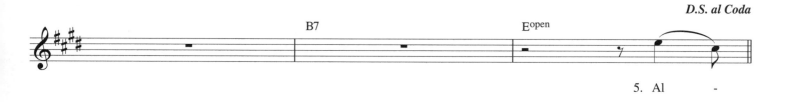

D.S. al Coda

5. Al -

we'll be so lone - ly, ba - by, well they're so lone - ly, ___

we'll be so lone - ly ____ they could die. _____

Don't Be Cruel
(To a Heart That's True)

Words and Music by Otis Blackwell and Elvis Presley

Don't Cry Daddy

Words and Music by Mac Davis

Additional Lyrics

2. Why are children always first
   To feel the pain and hurt the worst,
   It's true, but somehow it just don't seem right.
   'Cause ev'ry time I cry I know it hurts my little children so.
   I wonder will it be the same tonight.

Good Luck Charm

Words and Music by Aaron Schroeder and Wally Gold

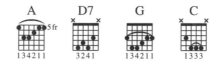

Intro

Moderately

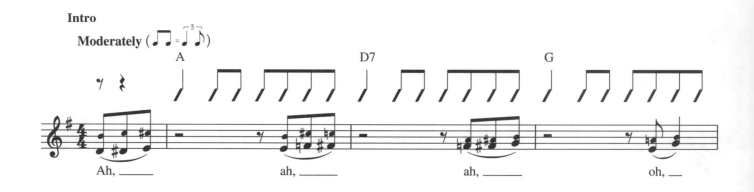

Ah, _____ ah, _____ ah, _____ oh, _____

Verse

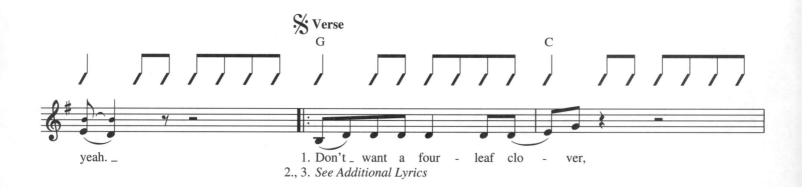

yeah. _

1. Don't _ want a four - leaf clo - ver,
2., 3. *See Additional Lyrics*

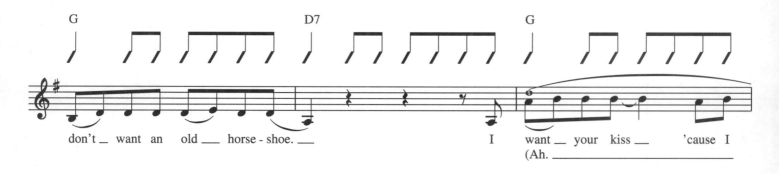

don't _ want an old _ horse - shoe. _ I want _ your kiss _ 'cause I
(Ah. _____

just _ can't miss with a good luck _ charm _ like _ you. Come on _ and
_)

Chorus

be my ___ lit - tle, ah, good luck charm, ___ ah, ___ ah, you sweet ___ de -

light. ___ I want a good luck charm ___ a hang - in' on ___ my arm, ah, to have,

To Coda

ah, to have, ah, to hold, ah, to hold, ah, to - night. ___

Interlude

Ah. ___ (Ah, ___) Ah. ___ (Ah. ___) Ah. ___
(Ah. ___) Ah. ___ (Ah. ___) Ah, to - night. ___

2nd time, D.S. al Coda   **Coda**

Outro

Oh, ___ yeah. ___ Ah, ___   Ah. ___ (Ah. ___) Ah. ___
3. If   (Ah. ___) Ah. ___

Repeat & fade

(Ah. ___) Ah. ___ (Ah. ___) Oh, ___ yeah. ___ Ah. ___
(Ah. ___) Ah, to - night. ___

Additional Lyrics

2. Don't want a silver dollar,
   Rabbit's foot on a string.
   The happiness and your warm caress,
   No rabbit's foot can bring.

3. If I found a lucky penny,
   I'd toss it across the bay.
   Your love is worth all the gold on Earth,
   No wonder that I say:

His Latest Flame

Words and Music by Doc Pomus and Mort Shuman

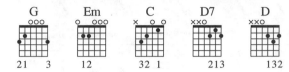

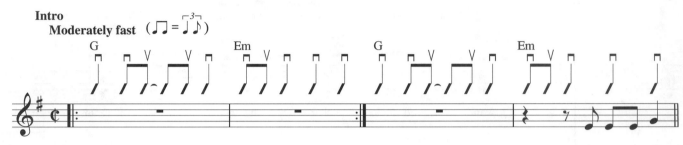

Intro
Moderately fast

1. A ver-y old

Verse

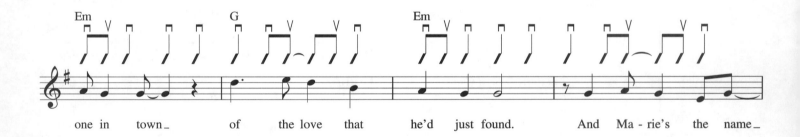

friend came by to-day, __ 'cause he was tell-in' ev-er-y
2. *See additional lyrics*

one in town __ of the love that he'd just found. And Ma-rie's the name __

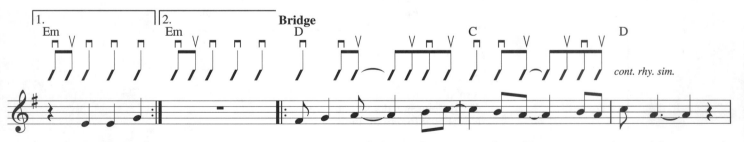

__ of his lat-est flame.

2. He talked and   Though I smiled, __ the tears __ in-side __ were a burn-in'. __

Additional Lyrics

2. He talked and talked, and I heard him say
That she had the longest, blackest hair,
The prettiest green eyes anywhere.
And Marie's the name of his latest flame.

Hound Dog

Words and Music by Jerry Leiber and Mike Stoller

Intro
Fast Rock

Chorus

You ain't noth-in' but a hound dog - a, c-cry-in' all the time.

You ain't _ noth-in' but a hound dog - a, cry-in' all the time.

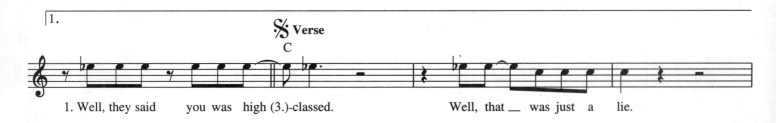

To Coda

Well, _ you ain't nev-er caught a rab-bit and you ain't no friend _ of mine. _

1. **Verse**

1. Well, they said you was high (3.)-classed. Well, that _ was just a lie.

Yeah, they said you was high - class. Well, that _ was just a lie.

Well, _ you ain't nev-er caught a rab-bit and you ain't no friend _ of mine. _

You ain't noth-in' but a

Guitar Solo

2. Well, they said you was high - classed. Well, that __ was just a

lie. Yeah, they said you was high - class. Well, that __ was just a

lie. Well, __ you ain't nev - er caught a rab - bit and you ain't no friend __ of mine. __

Guitar Solo

D.S. al Coda (take repeat)

3. Well, they said you was high -

Coda

nev - er caught a rab - bit; you

ain't no friend __ of mine. __ *Spoken:* You ain't noth-in' but a hound dog.

I Want You, I Need You, I Love You

Words by Maurice Mysels
Music by Ira Kosloff

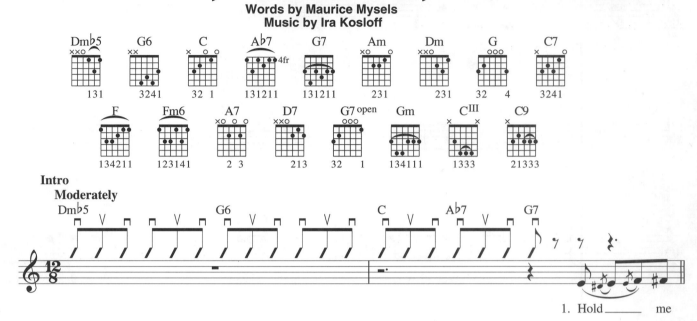

Intro
Moderately

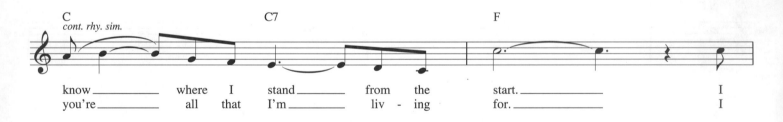

1. Hold _____ me

Verse

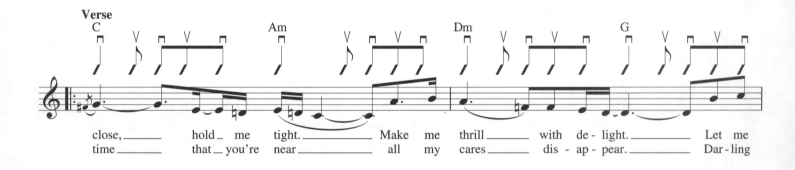

close, _____ hold me tight. _____ Make me thrill _____ with de - light. _____ Let me
time _____ that you're near _____ all my cares _____ dis - ap - pear. _____ Dar - ling

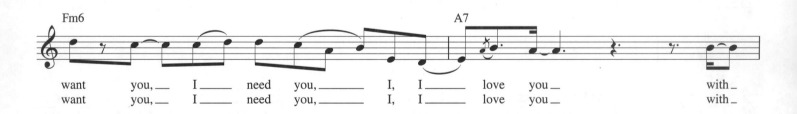

know _____ where I stand _____ from the start. _____ I
you're _____ all that I'm liv - ing for. _____ I

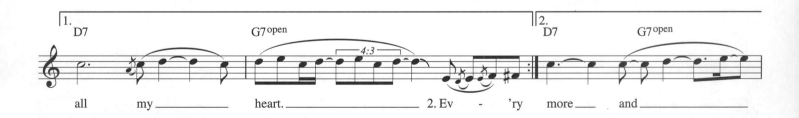

want you, __ I _____ need you, _____ I, I _____ love you __ with _____
want you, __ I _____ need you, _____ I, I _____ love you __ with __

1. all my _____ heart. _____ 2. Ev - 'ry more __ and _____

2.

In the Ghetto
(The Vicious Circle)
Words and Music by Mac Davis

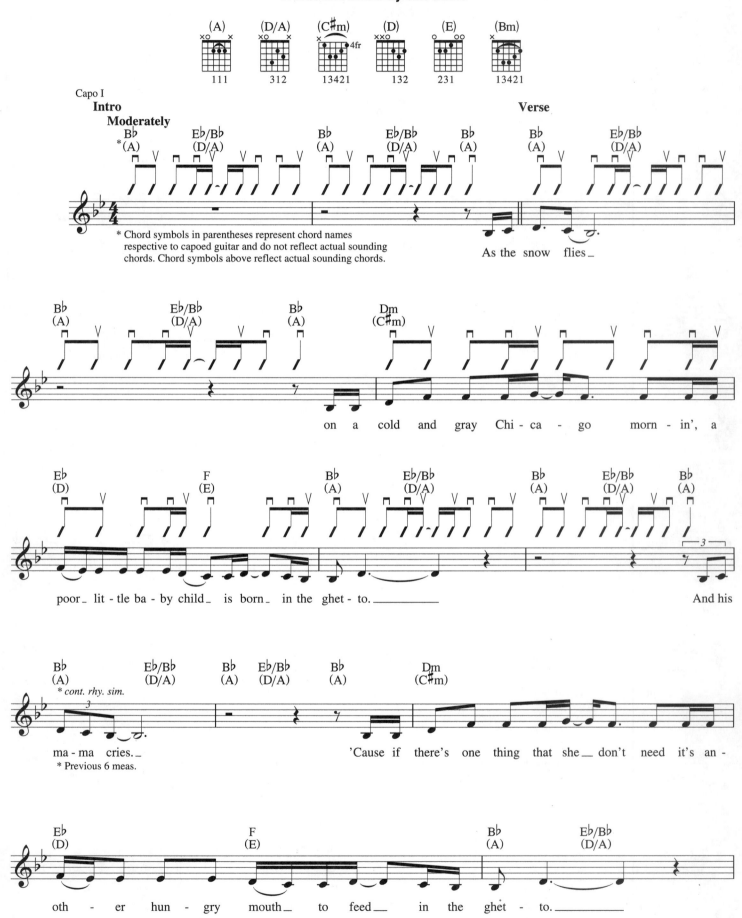

* Chord symbols in parentheses represent chord names respective to capoed guitar and do not reflect actual sounding chords. Chord symbols above reflect actual sounding chords.

As the snow flies on a cold and gray Chi-ca-go morn-in', a poor lit-tle ba-by child is born in the ghet-to. And his ma-ma cries. 'Cause if there's one thing that she don't need it's an-oth-er hun-gry mouth to feed in the ghet-to.

* Previous 6 meas.

down_ in the street with a gun_ in his hand_ in the ghet - to._____

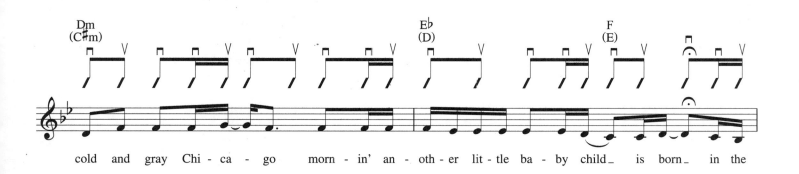

And as her young man_ dies____ on a

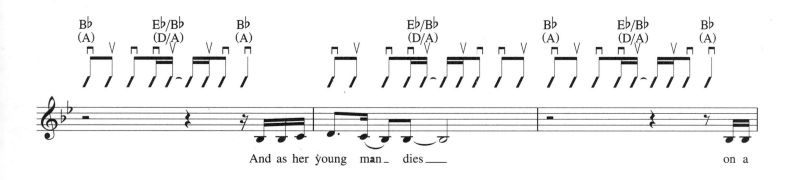

cold and gray Chi - ca - go morn - in' an - oth - er lit - tle ba - by child_ is born_ in the

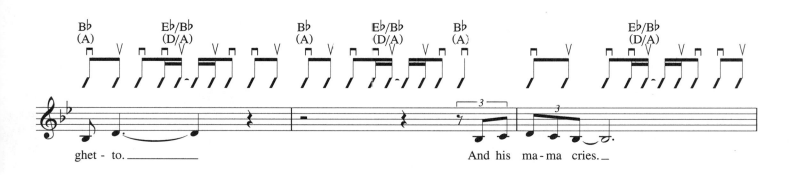

ghet - to._____ And his ma - ma cries._

Repeat and fade

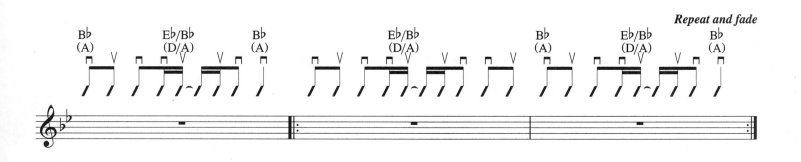

It's Now or Never
Words and Music by Aaron Schroeder and Wally Gold

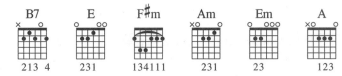

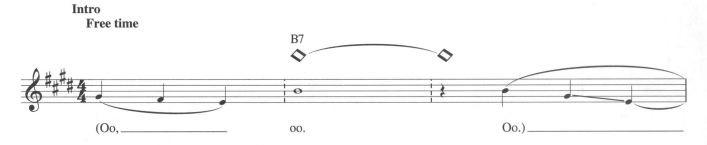

Intro
Free time

B7

(Oo, _____ oo. Oo.) _____

Moderately slow

𝄉 Chorus

E   E

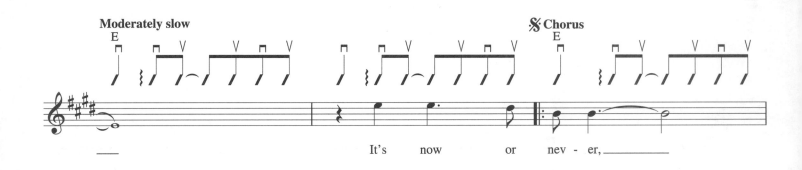

_____ It's now or nev-er, _____

cont. rhy. sim.   F#m

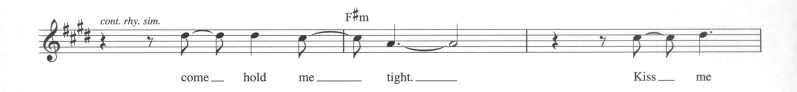

come __ hold me _____ tight. _____   Kiss __ me

B7   E

my dar-ling, __   be __ mine __ to-night. __

Am

To-mor-row _____ will _____ be

Em   E   B7

___ too late. ___ It's ___ now or ___ nev - er; ___

To Coda

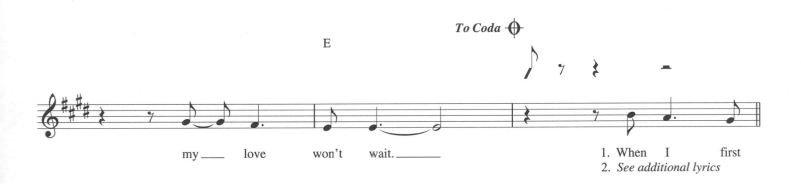

E

my ___ love won't wait. _____

1. When I first
2. *See additional lyrics*

Verse

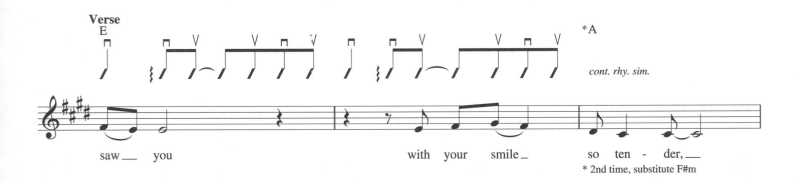

E   *A

cont. rhy. sim.

saw ___ you   with your smile ___ so ten - der, ___

* 2nd time, substitute F#m

B7

my ___ heart was ___ cap - tured;   my ___ soul

E

sur - ren - der. ___   I've ___ spent a life - time. ___

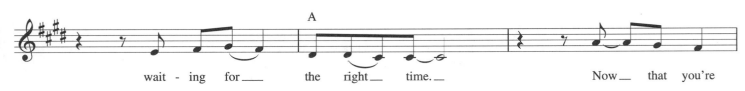

A

wait - ing for ___ the right ___ time. ___   Now ___ that you're

near, _____ the time is here _____ at _____ last. _____

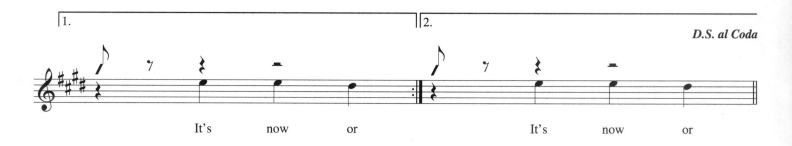

1. | **2.**

D.S. al Coda

It's now or It's now or

Coda

B7

It's now or _____ nev - er; _____ my love _____ won't _____

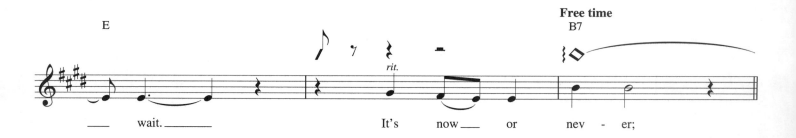

E **Free time**
B7
rit.

_____ wait. _____ It's now _____ or nev - er;

Moderately slow
E

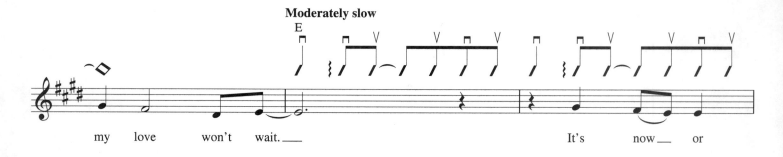

my love won't wait. _____ It's now _____ or

B7

E

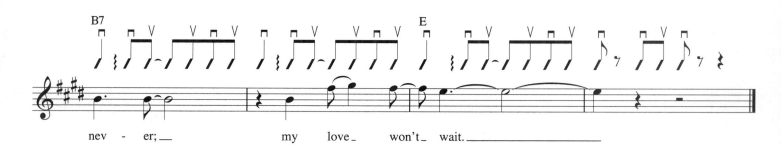

nev - er; _____ my love _ won't _ wait. _____

Additional Lyrics

2. Just like a willow, we would cry an ocean
If we lost true love and sweet devotion.
Your lips excite me; let your arms invite me.
For who knows when we'll meet again this way.

Stuck on You
Words and Music by Aaron Schroeder and J. Leslie McFarland

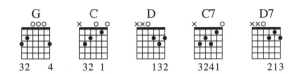

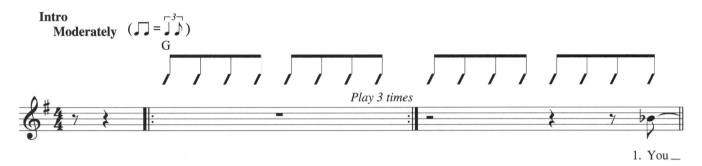

Intro
Moderately

Play 3 times

1. You___

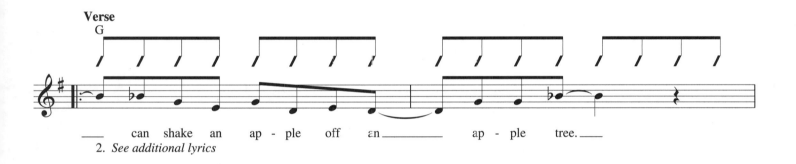

Verse

___ can shake an ap - ple off an ___ ap - ple tree. ___

2. *See additional lyrics*

cont. rhy. sim.

Shake - a shake - a sug - ar, but you'll nev - er shake me. ___ Uh, uh, uh. ___

No sir - ree, ___ uh, ___ uh. ___ I'm gon - na stick like glue. ___

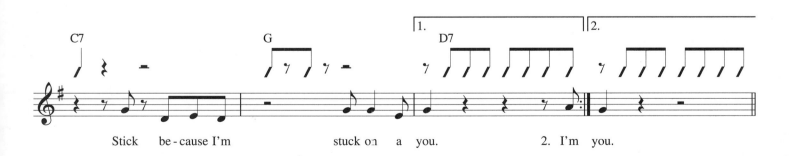

Stick be - cause I'm stuck on a you. 2. I'm you.

%. **Bridge**

Hide in the kitch- en, hide in the hall. Ain't gon - na do you no ____

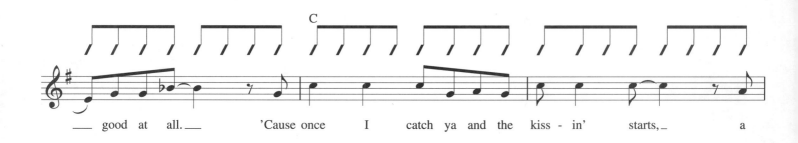

___ good at all. __ 'Cause once I catch ya and the kiss - in' starts, _ a

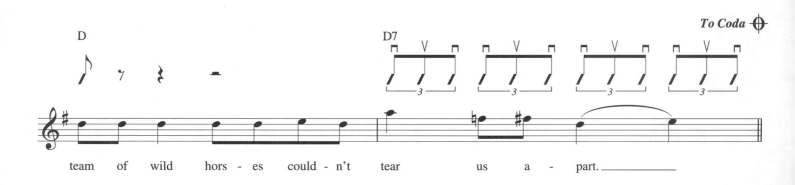

To Coda ⊕

team of wild hors - es could - n't tear us a - part. ____

Verse

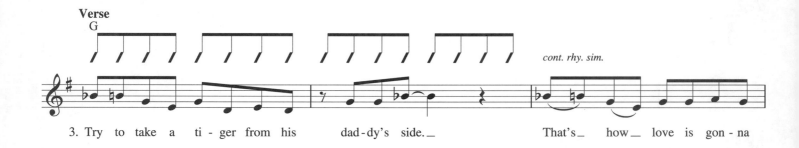

cont. rhy. sim.

3. Try to take a ti - ger from his dad - dy's side. _ That's _ how _ love is gon - na

keep us tied. _ Uh, huh, huh. ____ Uh, huh, huh. ____ Oh,

yeah. Uh, huh, huh. ___ I'm gon - na stick like glue. _

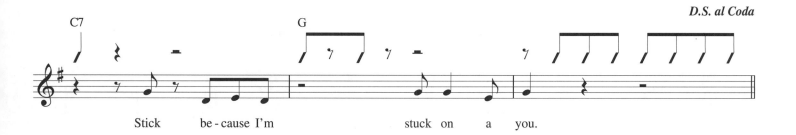

Stick be - cause I'm stuck on a you.

Coda
Outro-Verse

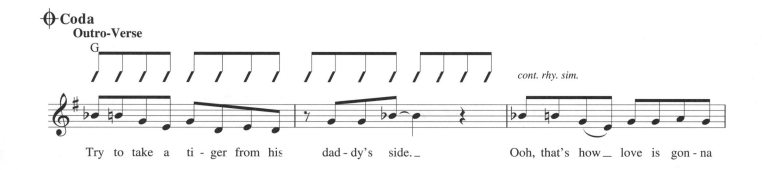

cont. rhy. sim.

Try to take a ti - ger from his dad - dy's side. ___ Ooh, that's how ___ love is gon - na

keep us tied. ___ Uh, huh, huh. _____ Yes sir - ee, _____ uh, huh. ___

I'm gon - na stick like glue. ___

Repeat and fade

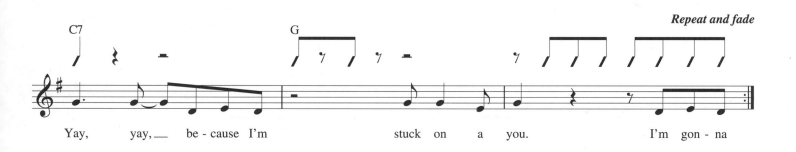

Yay, yay, ___ be - cause I'm stuck on a you. I'm gon - na

Additional Lyrics

2. I'm gonna squeeze my fingers through your long black hair,
   Squeeze you tighter than a grizzly bear.
   Uh, huh, huh. Yes siree uh, huh.
   I'm gonna stick like glue.
   Stick because I'm stuck on you.

Jailhouse Rock

Words and Music by Jerry Leiber and Mike Stoller

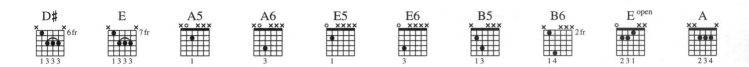

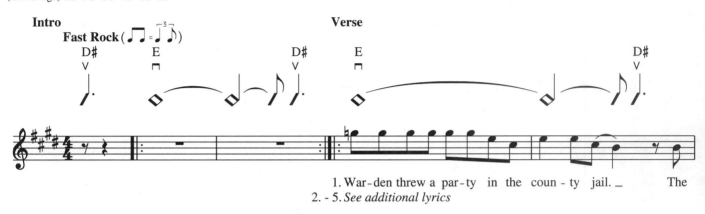

Tune down 1/2 step:
(low to high) Eb–Ab–Db–Gb–Bb–Eb

Intro
Fast Rock

Verse

1. War-den threw a par-ty in the coun-ty jail. _ The
2. - 5. *See additional lyrics*

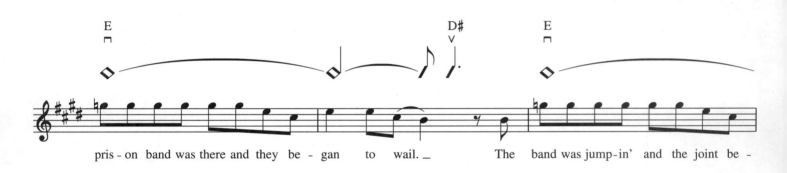

pris-on band was there and they be-gan to wail. _ The band was jump-in' and the joint be-

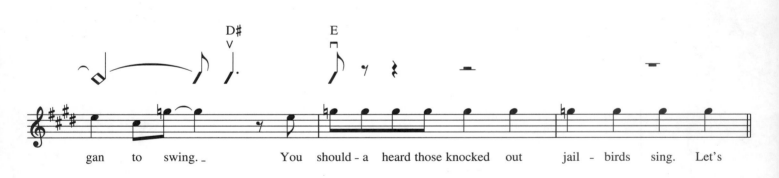

gan to swing. _ You should-a heard those knocked out jail-birds sing. Let's

Chorus

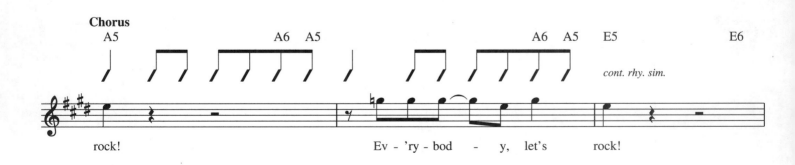

rock!   Ev-'ry-bod-y, let's rock!

Additional Lyrics

2. Spider Murphy played the tenor saxophone.
   Little Joe was blowin' on the slide trombone.
   The drummer boy from Illinois went crash, boom, bang.
   The whole rhythm section was the Purple Gang.

3. Number forty-seven said to number three,
   "You the cutest jailbird I ever did see.
   I sure would be delighted with your company.
   Come on, and do the Jailhouse Rock with me."

4. Sad Sack was sittin' on a block of stone,
   Way over in the corner weepin' all alone.
   The warden said, "Hey, buddy, don't you be no square.
   If you can't find a partner use a wooden chair."

5. Shifty Henry said to Bugs "For heaven's sake,
   No one's lookin', now's our chance to make a break."
   Bugs, he turned to Shifty and he said, "Nix, nix,
   I wanna stick around awhile to get my kicks."

Love Me Tender

Words and Music by Elvis Presley and Vera Matson

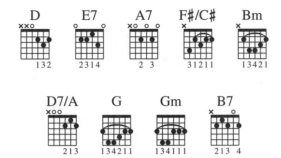

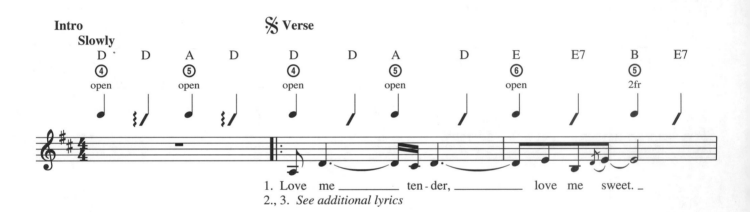

1. Love me _____ ten - der, _____ love me sweet.
2., 3. *See additional lyrics*

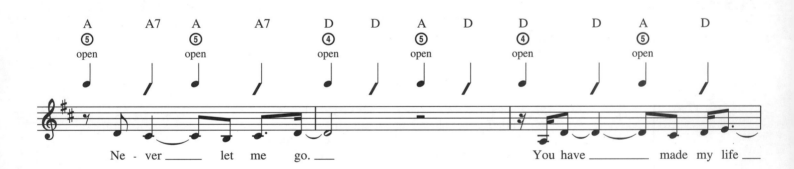

Ne - ver _____ let me go. _____ You have _____ made my life _____

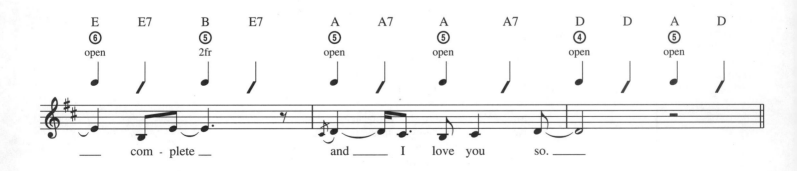

_____ com - plete _____ and _____ I love you so. _____

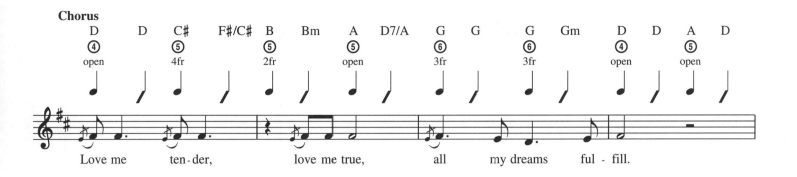

Chorus

Love me ten-der, love me true, all my dreams ful-fill.

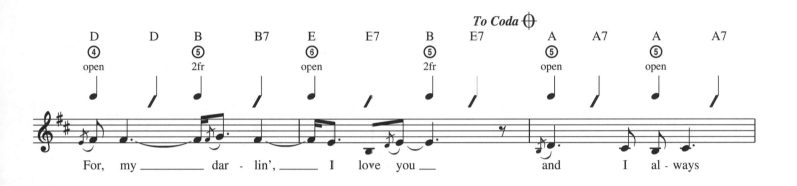

To Coda ⊕

For, my ___ dar-lin', ___ I love you ___ and I al-ways

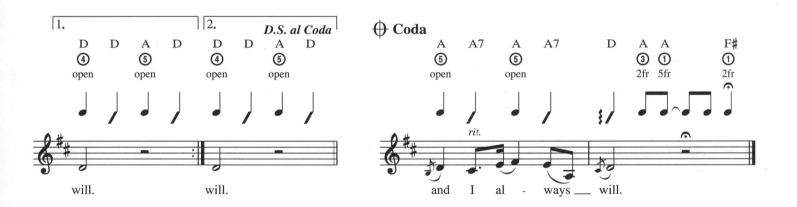

1. will.

2. *D.S. al Coda*
will.

⊕ **Coda**

and I al - ways ___ will.

Additional Lyrics

2. Love me tender, love me long.
   Take me to your heart.
   For it's there that I belong
   And we'll never part.

3. Love me tender, love me dear.
   Tell me you are mine.
   I'll be yours through all the years,
   'Til the end of time.

Return to Sender

Words and Music by Otis Blackwell and Winfield Scott

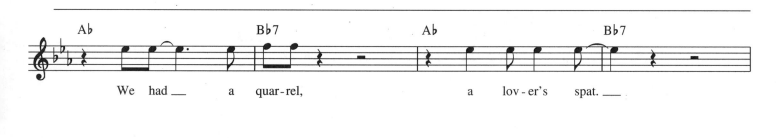

We had ___ a quar-rel, a lov-er's spat. ___

I write I'm sor-ry but my let-ter keeps com-ing back.

2.

Bridge

zone. This time ___ I'm gon-na take it my-self and put it right in her hand. And if it comes back the ver-y next day, ___ then I'll un-der-stand ___

Outro-Chorus

___ the writ-ing on it. Re - turn ___ to send - er,

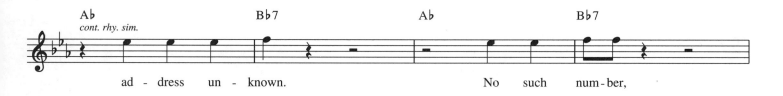

cont. rhy. sim.

ad - dress un - known. No such num - ber,

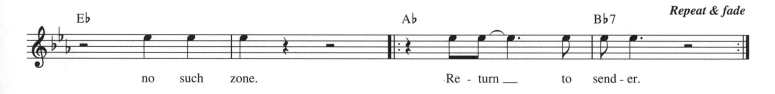

Repeat & fade

no such zone. Re - turn ___ to send - er.

Additional Lyrics

2. So then I dropped it in the mailbox
And sent it Special D.
Bright and early next morning.
It came right back to me.

Suspicious Minds

Words and Music by Francis Zambon

(Let Me Be Your)
Teddy Bear

Words and Music by Kal Mann and Bernie Lowe

Too Much

Words and Music by Lee Rosenberg and Bernie Weinman

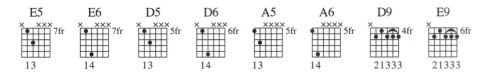

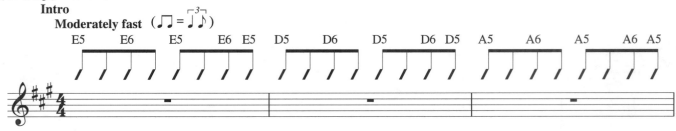

Tune down 1/2 step:
(low to high) E♭-A♭-D♭-G♭-B♭-E♭

Intro
Moderately fast

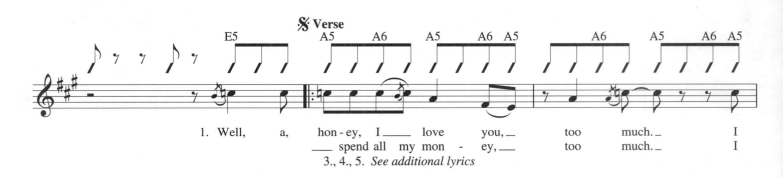

1. Well, a, hon-ey, I___ love you,___ too much.___ I
___ spend all my mon-ey,___ too much.___ I
3., 4., 5. *See additional lyrics*

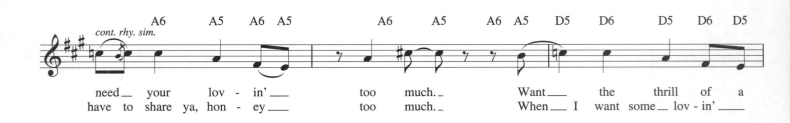

need___ your lov-in'___ too much.___ Want___ the thrill of a
have to share ya, hon-ey___ too much.___ When___ I want some___ lov-in'

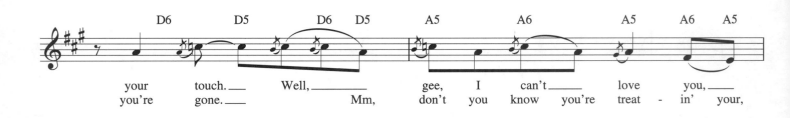

your touch.___ Well,_____ gee, I can't___ love you,___
you're gone.___ Mm, don't you know you're treat-in' your,

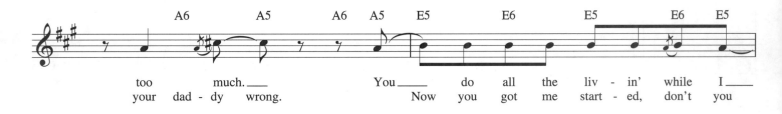

too much.___ You___ do all the liv-in' while I___
your dad-dy wrong. Now you got me start-ed, don't you

Additional Lyrics

3., 5. I need your lovin' all the time.
Need your huggin', please be mine.
Need you near me, stay real close.
Please, please hear me, you're the most.
Now you got me started,
Don't you leave me broken hearted.
Gonna love you too much.

4. Well, every time I kiss your sweet lips,
I can feel my heart go flip, flip.
I'm such a fool for your charms.
Take me back, my baby, in your arms.
Like to hear you sighin',
Even though I know you're lyin'.
Gonna love you too much.

Wear My Ring Around Your Neck

Words and Music by Bert Carroll and Russell Moody

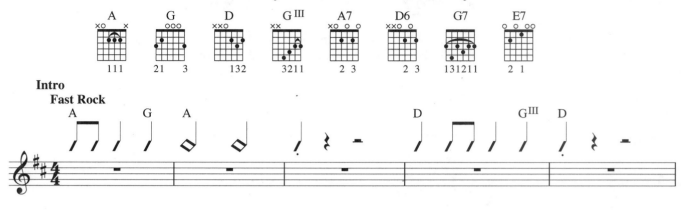

Intro
Fast Rock

% Verse

1. Won't you wear my (2., 3., 4.) ring up a - round your

neck, to tell the world__ I'm on - ly yours by

heck?__ Let__ them { 1., 3. see / 2., 4. know, }

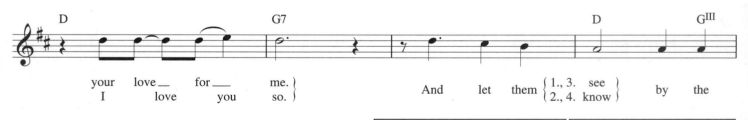

your love__ for__ me. }
I love you so. }
And let them { 1., 3. see / 2., 4. know } by the

1.   **2.**

4th time, to Coda ⊕

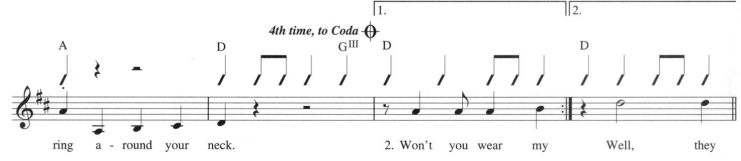

ring a - round your neck.   2. Won't you wear my   Well, they

Bridge

say that go-ing stead - y is not the prop-er thing.___ They

say that we're too young___ to know the mean-ing of a ring.___ I

on-ly know___ I love,___ love a you and a that you love___ a me, too. Oh

1st time, D.S.
(take 2nd ending)
2nd time, D.S. al Coda

dar - ling, this is a what I {ask / beg} of you. 3., 4. Won't you wear my

Coda

Outro

And let them know by the ring a - round your neck.

And let them know by the ring a - round___ your neck.___

Oh, yeah.

STRUM IT GUITAR LEGEND

Strum It is the series designed especially to get you playing (and singing!) along with your favorite songs. The idea is simple – the songs are arranged using their original keys in lead sheet format, providing you with the authentic chords for each song, beginning to end. Rhythm slashes are written above the staff. Strum the chords in the rhythm indicated. Use the chord diagrams found at the top of the first page of the arrangement for the appropriate chord voicings. The melody and lyrics are also shown to help you keep your spot and sing along.

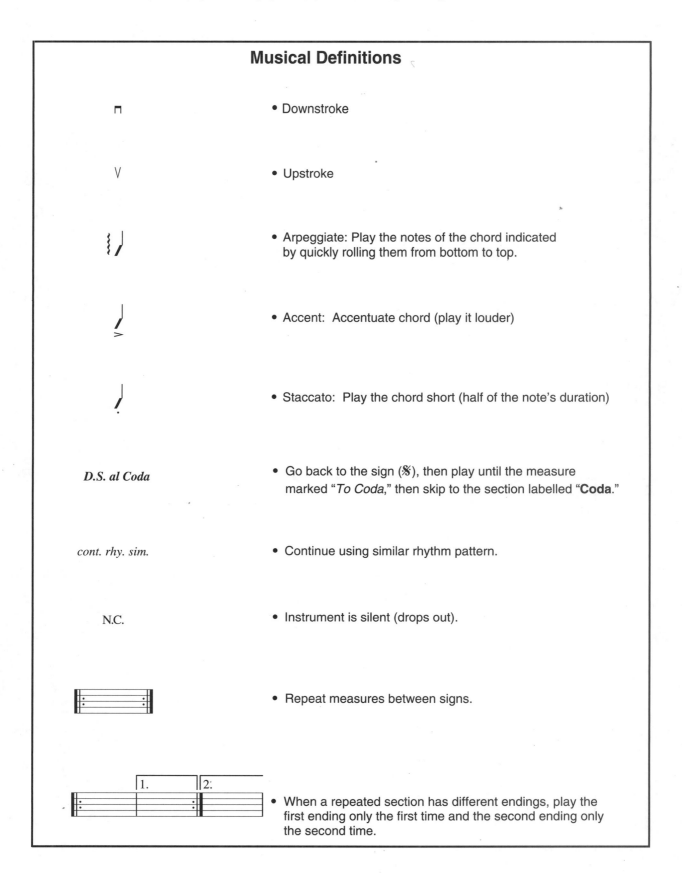

Musical Definitions

⊓	• Downstroke
V	• Upstroke
⌇♩	• Arpeggiate: Play the notes of the chord indicated by quickly rolling them from bottom to top.
♩>	• Accent: Accentuate chord (play it louder)
♩.	• Staccato: Play the chord short (half of the note's duration)
D.S. al Coda	• Go back to the sign (𝄋), then play until the measure marked "*To Coda*," then skip to the section labelled "**Coda**."
cont. rhy. sim.	• Continue using similar rhythm pattern.
N.C.	• Instrument is silent (drops out).
𝄆 𝄇	• Repeat measures between signs.
1. ‖ 2.	• When a repeated section has different endings, play the first ending only the first time and the second ending only the second time.